n*e*

The Day Nina Simone Stopped Singing

Darina Al Joundi is a critically acclaimed actor and writer of Lebanese-Syrian origin. The daughter of notorious Syrian journalist, freedom fighter, political activist and exile Assim Al Joundi, Darina Al Joundi is known throughout the Arab world for her television and film roles, and has also played occasional roles in popular English-language series such as Homeland and Tyrants.

Le Jour où Nina Simone a cessé de chanter (The Day Nina Simone Stopped Singing) was an instant sensation when Al Joundi first performed it as a one-woman play at the Avignon festival in July 2007: it sold out at every performance and resulted in multiple runs in Paris and throughout France. Al Joundi followed this up with the successful sequel *Ma Marseillaise* (Marseillaise My Way), which premiered at the Avignon festival in 2012.

Also by Darina Al Joundi

Novels
Le Jour où Nina Simone a cessé de chanter with Mohamed Kacimi
(Actes Sud, 2008)
Prisonnière du levant (Grasset, 2017)

Plays
Le Jour où Nina Simone a cessé de chanter (L'Avant-Scène Théâtre,
2012)
Ma Marseillaise (L'Avant-Scène Théâtre, 2012)

In translation
The Day Nina Simone Stopped Singing, novel, translated by
Marjolijn de Jager (Feminist Press, 2010)
Marseillaise My Way, play, translated by Helen Vassallo (Naked
Eye Publishing, 2022)
Prisoner of the Levant, translated by Helen Vassallo (Liverpool
University Press, forthcoming)

The Day Nina Simone Stopped Singing

a monologue

by

Darina Al Joundi

translated by *Helen Vassallo*

Naked Eye Publishing

First published in the French language as
'Le Jour où Nina Simone a cessé de chanter' by Darina Al
Joundi, L'Avant-Scène Théâtre, 2012

© Éditions L'Avant-Scène Théâtre, Collection des
quatre vents, 2012

© 2012, Darina Al Joundi

First published in English translation
by Naked Eye Publishing 2022

The poem by Hallaj is from 'Music of a Distant Drum: Classical
Arabic, Persian, Turkish and Hebrew Poems', translated by
Bernard Lewis (Princeton University Press, 2011), reproduced
here with kind permission of the publisher.

Book design and typesetting by Naked Eye

ISBN: 9781910981177

nakedeyepublishing.co.uk

CONTENTS

Preface

Noun is a part of me

I had never written before. Before my father died. He was a professor of philosophy and Arab literature, and it petrified me: the only time I had dared to write him a letter, he had sent it back to me with corrections marked in red ink. I stopped writing letters. Instead I used my acting as a kind of writing. It's my way of understanding and performing my roles. I have always used my life and my own experiences to give depth to the characters I play. It's my way of transforming my life into a source of inspiration for my art: everything becomes positive and interesting – the joys, but also the sorrows and tears. When my father passed away in 2001 and I was beaten up and locked away in an asylum, I thought of one thing only: once I got out of there, I would do everything I could to leave and tell my story on stage. Because while it was happening to me, I couldn't believe what I was living through. I kept saying to myself: it's a film, a play, it's a story that has to be told. Suddenly I looked differently at myself and at what was happening around me. Every detail, every colour, every sound, every smell had a different meaning. But this play is not a therapy through performance. It could have been, if it had been the first time that I stepped out on a stage inventing myself as an actress, and told my life story on stage as a form of therapy. All my life I've only ever been an actress. With Noun, I created a character in a play. Noun is not me, but she is a part of me. A part that I love and that life and society will no longer tolerate: she isn't allowed to shout loud and clear what she thinks in real life, but at the theatre she's applauded for it.

Noun and this play gave me the opportunity to discover France.

Karine, Carole and me, travelling around France for more than three years. We had some unforgettable times on the road, on the trains, in the various hotels. And especially in the theatres! With all the wonderful teams who welcomed us, and the amazing audiences that I'll never forget. Towns, villages, places I would never have dreamed of. And the adventures we had getting there! We got lost almost every time we went somewhere new, in spite of all the maps, GPS and satnavs we had on us. Touring with the play gave me the opportunity to discover a France that I would never have had the fortune or the pleasure to discover alone. Otherwise how would I ever have made it to Villefranche-de-Rouergue or Chênehutte-Trèves-Cunault, or my personal favourite: Condom-sur-Baïse! So many unforgettable encounters with interested and inquiring audiences who showered me with so much love during each show!

People often asked me after the show: "What's the poem you recite at the end? Is it one of your father's?" I would reply "It's a poem my father used to recite to me. At the end of the play, I offer it back to him." I promised to translate it when the play was published: I have kept my promise here.

Darina Al Joundi

The night after her father's funeral, Noun interrupts the prayers of the Qur'an. Staying true to the memory of her father, a writer, journalist and freedom fighter, she locks herself in a room with his body and spends one last night with him. To the soundtrack of Nina Simone, Noun tells the story of her childhood in Lebanon. She talks about the war, the stranglehold of religion, the weight of prejudice, and her struggle against a society where men are all-powerful and women are denied freedom of speech.

1.

Noun is sitting alone, in a hand-drawn square of white chalk. On the stage the lights are down; in the auditorium they are up. She is waiting for the audience to arrive. In her head she is thinking "I've been waiting for you for a long time. I'm going to tell you what happened to me. I've been waiting for this moment for years now". She knows that, in telling them her story, she will be free. People start coming into the theatre and take their seats.

Sitting on the stage floor, Noun watches them, visibly happy to see them and smiling as they come in. When everyone is seated, she says:

"I had almost given up on you!"

She smiles at them. She has said the first sentence, the one that says first and foremost that she is there in front of them and has already won her struggle, this struggle that she's going to tell them about. She thinks about what she's going to say to them. She sits silently, making eye contact with the audience. The lights go down slowly.

The theatre is in darkness.

In the darkness, Noun stands up. She is happy that she's going to tell them her story. Then the voice of Nina Simone singing

'Sinnerman' rings out. Suddenly, Noun remembers her father. He was the one who introduced her to the music of Nina Simone, and taught her to love Simone's songs, especially 'Sinnerman'. The song fades from her head and from the room; she can hear her father calling to her.

The lights go up.

Noun snaps out of her reverie, and sees the audience in front of her. She remembers that she is there to speak to them, to tell them what happened. The first thing she has to tell them is that her father is dead. She has never yet said this out loud; she can't quite bring herself to say it. She tries to speak, but her voice catches in her throat. She does not want to say it, because she does not want to accept that it has happened. She struggles to contain her emotions, and then cries out:

My father died the day he thought he had no more stories to tell me.

She realises what she has just said. It's the first time she has said out loud that her father is dead. She pulls herself together: she has to tell the story. She takes a few steps forward, and looks at the audience. And suddenly it's as if she were seeing images, a scene played out in front of her.

I'm with his body now. He's naked, in the middle of the room, covered with a simple...

She sees her father as clearly as if he were there with her, and cannot accept that he ended up like this, against his wishes. All the rage inside her comes out, rage against death, especially her father's death.

...white shroud!

She turns away from the audience; she knows she must contain her rage. She turns back towards them and carries on describing the scene.

He's lying on his back, hands folded across his crotch. Looking at him, he seems so peaceful.

At this point, she remembers. She comes back to the moment and speaks to the audience. She is angry – angry with her father. She calls on the audience to witness.

It's the first time in my life that I've seen him at peace. I'm not sad that he's gone. I'd known for a long time that he was going to die because he'd already told me everything!

She falls silent, thinking: "No, he hadn't told me everything, not yet." She relives the sorrow all over again, the sorrow of never again hearing everything he had to share with her. But now is not the time. She must carry on with her story. She raises her head to speak, and sees the scenes before her eyes again.

Through the open window, I can see the houses of my village, Arnoun, "the Fortress of Beaufort". There's still smoke rising from the bombed-out houses. The Israeli army has just withdrawn from Southern Lebanon after twenty years of occupation. I can see the surrounding hills, teeming with people. They've come from Tyr, Sidon, Damascus, Aleppo, Beirut and Amman to attend my father's funeral.

Dear God, it's true, this funeral is really happening. How is she going to get through it? She sees him before her, as if it were the day of the funeral.

I stroke his face, it's so soft, not even cold.

She can still feel his skin against her hand.

It's January. It's raining. I can smell the scent of the rain rising up from the red earth of Southern Lebanon.

She turns around as if she's heard a noise. She bursts out laughing; she's living through it again.

The door opens. Women dressed in black come pouring in. They're weeping and wailing. They hurl themselves on my father: they kiss his face. They kiss his hands. They kiss his feet as if they wanted to gobble him up! I whisper in his ear: "You sly dog, you don't miss a trick do you!"

She bursts out laughing at the memory of the women throwing themselves on her father's corpse. She turns her head.

Suddenly, I hear a strange voice that chills me to the bone. An unbearable moan that cuts right through me. A wail that lashes at my skin and hacks at my skull: someone is howling out verses from the Qur'an.

She says the word 'Qur'an' in Arabic; there is a silence, and then she looks her audience straight in the eye, as if to make them understand the word, and she says it again with an English accent. Beyond the edge of the stage, she sees herself back in that room.

I open the door to the next room. It's full of weeping women dressed in black, all huddled around a cassette player that's spitting out the prayers. I push past them all, trampling on them. I grab hold of the cassette player and turn it off. The women cry out in horror. My mother and my sisters try to hold me back:
"Stop it, what's wrong with you? Get back, now's not the time..."
I run away from them, into my father's room, and deadlock the heavy oak door. I can hear my brother-in-law pounding on it, shouting:
"You crazy bitch, put the Qur'an back on or I'll kill you! Open up, bitch, open the door! No-one cuts short the word of God. Open up, you little whore, no-one touches the Holy Book"
Don't you lay a finger on me! He hasn't even been buried yet and…

She doesn't know what to do. Her father is dead. He's gone. She calls out to her brother-in-law again.

He's not my father's God! My father never even had a God. He made me promise him: "Noun, make sure those bastards don't stick on the Qur'an at my funeral. Noun, promise me, put on jazz at my funeral, maybe even hip-hop, but definitely no Qur'an."

She hears someone beating at the door. It's her brother-in-law again. She thinks he might break down the door.

There's no point breaking the door down!

They're still pounding at the door, she can hear the noise in her head even now: Boom! Boom! Boom!

Are you still at it? I'll play Nina Simone for him, Miles Davis, Fairouz, even Mireille Mathieu, but not the Qur'an! Do you hear me, you bastard?

She shouts out expletives in Arabic that mean 'asshole', 'pimp', 'dog', 'jackass', 'shithead', 'lowlife', 'scum', 'moron', 'criminal' and 'maniac'.

Stop hammering like that! I won't open the door. I'm staying here, I'm going to sleep beside him.

Emotion overwhelms her, but she struggles against it. She doesn't want to get upset, she wants to fight.

You're not going to bury him like that, you'll never get him. I'll never open this door!"

She starts singing, shouting out Nina Simone's 'Save Me'. The soundtrack of the song joins in with her voice, and she carries on singing with Nina Simone. It's a cry for help: she is fighting through her singing and dancing. In singing the song, she feels her father is back with her.

She dances and sings, then, out of breath, addresses her father:

I'm singing for you, Pappa. Are you happy now? You've had your Nina Simone, you've had your jazz, I've saved you from the Qur'aaaaaaaaan!

The music stops. It's as though he's there, in front of her. She's afraid, she curls up on the floor, exhausted.

And now what am I going to do? Who's going to protect me from your son-in-law? That monster! You're the one who warned me: "Watch out, Noun, the men in this country are monsters towards women. They're hung up on appearances, they're slaves to their customs, they're nuts about God, they're tied to their mother's apron strings, and they're obsessed with money. They spend their lives offering up their arses to God on a platter. They unzip their flies as if they were arming a machine gun. They let their dicks loose on women as if they were unleashing pitbulls. They're dogs!"

She's exhausted. Lying on the ground, she talks to her father.

Now that you're no longer here, who am I going to hang out with? Who am I going to have fun with? I'm sure you're laughing at being locked up again.

She comes out of her little bubble with her father, and comes back to the audience. She sits down and starts talking to them.

You know, he spent half his life in prisons across the Arab world. When my mother was pregnant with me, he was wasting away in a prison in Damascus. When I was born, he was in jail in Palmyra. When I took my first steps, he was in exile in Africa. On my tenth birthday, he was under house arrest in Baghdad. At 15, I waited for his release outside the police station in Amman, then at 18 I tagged along when he was banished to Cyprus. And on my 20th birthday I knocked at every prison door in Syria to find him.

She starts to realise what she's saying. This is her life story she's telling. She loves her life. She remembers these moments, she remembers all those times she spent with him. She remembers her childhood being joyful, even though it was marked by imprisonment, exile and going on the run.

Happy times! Those were the good old days. Ah, the Orient, the voice of the muezzin, the Umayyad Mosque, the smells of the souks, the after-dinner shisha, sweet mint tea, pistachios from Aleppo, belly dancing, and the baklava at St Thomas's Gate... so good I swear you'd sell your soul for them.

People have only ever wanted to see these Eastern clichés in the home that she loves so dearly. But as far as Noun is concerned, her father and those like him were thrown to the dogs for standing up to the totalitarian regime. She turns to the audience to ask a question.

What did they have against him, all those spooks in Lebanon, Iraq, Syria and Jordan? He was guilty of being a writer! A journalist who wrote what he wanted.

She turns back to the place where she had been talking to her father and felt his presence. It was as if he never really understood those regimes at all... he carried on wanting to fight for freedom, for democracy... How could he think he could have freedom of speech with all that was going on around him? With all the contradictions that he saw every day? She addresses him again.

You never got it, Pappa!...

She turns back to the audience.

What shocked him the most was always ending up in cell number five. In Amman, in Damascus, in Baghdad... That's what you call oriental universalism! Even in Beirut, the "free city"… he wasn't allowed to write or to sign his work with his own name, he wrote anonymously just to put food on the table. To make sure we were okay even if he didn't see us much.

Yes, she remembers, it's true, she didn't see him much. What with him always fighting a cause, being exiled, or being on the run, she never really spent much time with him. She talks to her father again.

Just now, one of your old mistresses kissed your hands. I told her she should try kissing your dick. You never know, there could have been some life in the old dog yet. She might have raised you from the dead. She could have been Jesus, and you… Lazarus!

The room goes dark, and Nina Simone's 'Sinnerman' picks up from where it left off at the start of the show. She sings along with Nina Simone, shouting out the lyrics with her. When the lights go up again, she is facing the audience.

2.

The lights come back up. Noun is smiling, waiting to begin her story.

I've been waiting for you to tell you this story. A true story. My story. Five years I wore black to mourn my father.

She sees herself over those five years. She wore nothing but black the whole time. It was her way of hitting back, of reminding everyone that her father was gone.

Today I've put on a red dress for you. My father never ran with the crowd. He was a free spirit. He was born in 1933 in Salamiyah, in Syria. It was a city filled with poets, writers and communists… a city where people sat at the feet of Aristotle and Plato instead of Jesus or Mohammed. When he was 20, he moved away to Lebanon, to teach literature and philosophy. It was the golden age, all the writers and artists of the day had made their way to Beirut. Beirut was a free city, a haven for all the intellectuals who had no freedom of speech in their own country.

Talking about these times, her face lights up because those were the days when she would always see her father. Happy days, days when the house was full of people.

When he met my mother, also a journalist, they'd go out together and paint the town red. He never hid his wife away. He wrote thirteen novels and all his poems on café terraces. I was born on the 25th of February 1968 in Beirut.

She remembers the detail that is most important for her.

My dad wasn't there when I was born, he had just gone underground to help free Palestine!

She smiles bitterly. No, he wasn't there when she was born. But he lost everything. He ended up in prison…

I remember the day he came home. I was in my bedroom, I'd just turned three, and suddenly a man came in. He was quite tall, and just starting to lose his hair. He threw his arms around me and I ran away in tears. That was my dad. He never forgot the first time we met. We lived in a big house, my parents, my two sisters and me, in Ain el-Remanneh, right in the middle of the Christian district. My father was devoutly secular. All his life, he made sure he only lived in Christian neighbourhoods and only sent us to Catholic schools. He liked Jesus. He used to compare him to Che Guevara. He thought Jesus was handsome and used to say that anyone who turned water into wine couldn't be all that bad. When I was five years old, my father, ever more secular, sent me to the Holy Family convent school. He had never told me if I was Christian or Muslim. I loved Bible classes. I especially liked the story about the stoning of the whore. I was always in the front row, and I loved going to church. I used to inhale the incense, I couldn't get enough of it, and I never missed a single Mass in classical Arabic or in Latin.

The day before the civil war broke out, the nuns decided to separate the Christian pupils from the Muslim ones. I was just running off to go to Bible class when Sister Marie-Thérèse grabbed my collar and pulled me back:

"You're a Muslim. You can't go to Bible class".

I was very sad. I didn't understand why all of a sudden I was a Muslim. I begged her:

"Please Sister, let me go to class, I eat all the communion wafers you know, no-one ever wants them and I eat them all! Please, Sister, I scoff Jesus at every Mass!"

The nun took pity on me.

"And why do you want to go to Bible class so badly? Do you love our Lord so very much?"

I replied without thinking:

"Yes Sister, I love the Bible, it's even better than the *Arabian Nights*!"

She pushed me away as hard as she could:

"You're a Muslim alright! No more Bible class for you!"

I got my revenge: I peed in the font.

3.

The theatre is in darkness. Nina Simone's 'Sinnerman' picks up again. Once again, Noun lets herself go, breathing and singing with Nina Simone, shouting out the words of the song. The lights go up, and Noun walks forward towards the audience.

We were living in East Beirut, on Pierre Gemayel Street. It was a Sunday. I heard gunshots, screams, shouting. On the bridge opposite I saw a bus in flames. My mother came running in through the door, terrified, she had seen the Phalangists force forty-seven Palestinians off the bus…

Noun finds it hard to describe the scene.

to kill them. It was the 13th of April 1975, civil war had just broken out in Lebanon. One evening, while we were having dinner, we heard the president, Suleiman Frangieh, giving a speech on Radio Monte Carlo Middle East.

She picks up a statue of President Frangieh, and mimicks what she heard on the radio that day:

"Lebanese Christians are in grave danger. I have asked our Syrian brothers to come and save us".

She is still shocked by these words, and she remembers her father's reaction.

My father stood up from the table:

"The assassins are coming back".

Her father would have to flee the country now; she sees him before her, and describes the scene.

In the night he packed his bags and went to Baghdad.

"I'll see you soon my loves, I'm off to Iraq. I'll set up a free radio station, and we'll bring down the Syrian dictatorship. We'll start a revolution".

She remembers all that they went through in those times, and the disappointment that awaited them in Baghdad. Revolution… in a city where there was no such thing as freedom. She explains why she has kept quiet about it until now, and why she had been so disappointed.

In Baghdad, it wasn't the done thing to live in an apartment block. People used to say that only criminals and whores lived in apartment blocks. And my father rented us an apartment, in a block right on the Tigris… As secular as ever, my dad enrolled my sisters and me in the Jewish school in Baghdad. We were the only goys in the school. I loved it there. It was like one long music class. One evening, we were shown a screening of *The Ten Commandments* with Charlton Heston dubbed into classical Arabic. I wept when I heard Charlton Heston shouting at God in classical Arabic:

She sees all the children sitting down watching the film. She recites Charlton Heston's speech dubbed into Arabic. She sees her audience and goes up to them to explain what she has just said.

"Oh! This people have sinned a great sin, and have made them gods of gold. Yet now, if thou wilt, forgive their sin, and if not, blot me, I pray thee, from thy book which thou hast written".

I felt I was ready to understand the mystery of faith. I asked my father what a believer was.

She imitates her father's response:

"A believer, my dear, is a ball-breaker who makes other people's lives hell to get to heaven".

She laughs, proud of her father's response. She is reliving those moments and that makes her happy. She goes back to her story.

One night, two men knocked at the door. They were Iraqi Secret Service. One of them said to me:

"Wake your father up, we're taking him for a coffee".

Saddam had just come to power. Before they locked up my dad, he said to us:

"I won't leave you at the mercy of these lunatics. I'm sending you back to Beirut tomorrow. I've enrolled you at Saint Joseph's school, with the nuns. They're left-wingers".

She laughs again. She sees all these images before her, She sees all these images before her, and her dad speaking so seriously…

And so off I went to the left-wing nuns. They were always closing the school so that we could go on marches with the Lebanese Communist party. I can still remember the banners I used to wave:

"Comrades, the nuns of Saint-Joseph's school are with you!"

That was Lebanon!

Her smile fades, and her joy along with it… She remembers that this Lebanon, one where nuns could stand shoulder to shoulder with communists, no longer exists. She knows she must continue telling her story, and she comes back to the moment.

In 1979, the Iraqis set my father free.

"Don't worry my love, one day we'll have our revolution. You'll see Noun, one day all women will be free to have sex with whoever they want. We'll turn all their mosques and churches into brothels".

More laughter, more of the funny things her father used to say. She always loved listening to her father, because of the way he used to explain things, analysing the terms and words that he used. She speaks to the audience again, and carries on trying to describe her father to them.

He always liked having an open house in Beirut. All the poets, musicians, philosophers and filmmakers in the city used to come to our house. Every night was a celebration, alcohol flowed freely, and poetry too. My sister and I used to put on shows for all the guests.

She can see the living room now, and all the people gathered in it.

There were books everywhere. Rimbaud rubbed shoulders with Lenin, Gibran was propped up against Lacan, Sartre and Ibn Khaldoun were never far apart… he brought me up on Baudelaire, the Arab erotic poets, the sufis, and Hallaj.

She recites a poem by Hallaj, one that her father always loved.

"I am the One whom I love, and the One whom I love is myself.
We are two souls incarnated in one body;
if you see me, you see Him,

if you see Him, you see us".

She twirls around as she recites the poem, as if she were herself having a moment of sufi enlightenment. Exhausted and a little dizzy, she collapses on the ground, and when she comes round she seems a little disorientated.

My sister had a beautiful voice, like Fairouz. A TV producer gave her a spot on his show; my father insisted that I should go with her. There she was singing live on TV and I, just turned ten, played the cheeky little sister. I raised merry hell on set! That evening the producer came up to offer us a contract for the whole series. By the tender age of ten I was famous throughout Lebanon and I was even financially independent.

She stands up, proud of being financially independent since the age of ten. She takes a few steps, remembering the television sets of her childhood, the shoots and an important day in her young life. She looks at the audience and lets them into a secret.

I got my first period on a TV set. Back then my dad used to write a column in a daily newspaper. He loved writing about our life. The next day, I came across the morning issue of the *Revolutionary Front*, and in it he'd written an article saying: "First thing tomorrow, I'm off to buy Tampax for my daughter!"

She bursts out laughing.

I remember I was wearing a little lilac dress. Lilac was his favourite colour. I was very well developed for my age and I used to try to hide it, I had proper boobs and he thought it was hilarious. One day I said to him,

She takes a few steps towards the audience, stops, and speaks in a determined voice:

"Pappa, I want you to buy me a bra. A white one."

He was furious, like I'd never seen him before: "Are you crazy? Do you have a screw loose? Is the war not enough for you, now you want a bra as well? Don't you know that a bra is a hideous contraption that will stop you breathing, and practically strangle you? You have no idea how awful it is... when a woman gets undressed and suddenly you see the mark that the straps have left on her shoulders! No, don't do it, not you, Noun. The worst of all is the indent the clasp makes in your back. You're with your lover, he's running his hands over your body, his finger passes over it, and it's like suddenly there's a pothole in the middle of your back. No, Noun, you must never wear a bra".

She smiles.

I got my way in the end. We went to the Saint Elias souk.

She remembers the walk they took together that day.

We chose the bra together. My dad asked the saleslady to teach him all the sizes.

She can see him now, teasing the saleslady who was showing him the bras and teaching him the sizes, cupping their hands to learn the different sizes.

32A, 34B, 36C, 40D.

He was such a joker! She bursts out laughing.

I went home so proud of my new bra, I felt like I was a proper woman now. I was so proud that I wanted to go to bed with it on.

She remembers that moment, that night.

In the middle of the night I woke up half-choking. I could hardly move or breathe. It was like an iron collar, I felt like I was going to suffocate. I pulled it off and threw it out of the window.

She looks straight at the audience.

I haven't worn one since.

The lights go down, and Nina Simone's 'Sinnerman' plays again. Noun sings along.

4.

The lights go up. Noun is back in her white square, holding a bottle of whisky and swigging from it. She swallows her first mouthful, and starts to talk.

I was obsessed with the concept of virginity…

She sits down.

…the only asset an Arab girl can have. What should I do with it?

She explains what she means.

For me, virginity is like the seal on a jar of Gold Blend. A gay friend once told me you have to pop it yourself, otherwise all Arab women are condemned to finish their days with the man who broke their seal. In Lebanon they say 'devirginise'. I devirginise, you devirginise… how stressful! So I decided to do it myself. At midnight I called my father, who was living in

Nicosia at the time, to tell him what I was going to do:

She speaks as though she were her father.

"You're right Noun, you know what they say in Lebanon, 'I popped her open'. As if women were bottles. Can you see yourself cuddling up with a man who'd pop you open like a bottle of beer?

She smiles, proud of herself.

No sooner had he said it than I closed my eyes, took a deep breath, and pushed my finger inside myself as hard as I could. I felt blood on my hand and started breathing again. I said "I'm free, Pappa". And I hung up.

She takes a swig of whisky and then remembers something else.

It was wartime, the madness was just beginning, it hadn't quite hit us yet. We drank a lot, and we smoked constantly. Since I hadn't yet found anyone to fall in love with, I pretended to be infatuated with Nabil, a motorbike-loving cousin of mine. We used to dance the java together. One night, battle was raging on the demarcation line, and he said I could wait at his place until the shooting died down. Once we were in his apartment, he opened a bottle of whisky. Since there was no electricity, we had no ice.

She sees the whole scene clearly before her eyes.

He polished off half a bottle of Johnnie Walker in one glug.

She turns suddenly, as if she had heard a noise.

I could hear the bombs going off. He lay me down on the sofabed.

She can still feel that sofabed with its beige velvet cover. She looks out at the audience.

Through the windows I could see flare bombs tearing up the sky over Beirut.

She can see the lights, and she's fascinated by them. But something is bothering her. She feels as though she's suffocating.

He was panting on top of me, I tried to wriggle away, but he crushed his hands around my neck and screamed:

"Don't you move, I know you're not a virgin, you're not a virgin!"

After screaming these words, she continues.

The sky was ablaze over Beirut. His fingernails were digging into my throat. He came inside me and then fell at my feet, drunk as a skunk.

She has another swig of whisky.

I ran out of there as fast as I could, it was 2am but no-one stopped me in the street, there were no more roadblocks but there were soldiers everywhere, all drugged up to the eyeballs. I was crying in the street. All that waiting around for love and that was it?

And now she remembers what her father had told her about love, and reality hits her.

I could feel his sperm running down my thighs… Back home, my mum was still awake, she had been waiting up for me. I couldn't tell her what had happened, I didn't want her to know. I went for a shower and I stayed there for an hour, scrubbing myself until I bled.

She can hear the shower and feel the hot water, feel her skin ripping away from her. She sees an image of herself.

My hair was wet, I opened a bottle of red wine and went to sit at my father's desk. I don't know how, but I knew I was going to fall pregnant that night.

She remembers that feeling. It's true, she knew that she was going to fall pregnant.

I picked up the phone to call my dad in Nicosia and wake him up to tell him.

It's as if she wanted to unleash all her fury on him.

But I didn't make the call. I could put him through just about anything, but not that. He wouldn't have been able to bear it. Since abortion is illegal in Lebanon, I reported the rape.

She sees herself in the hospital.

I spent my fifteenth birthday at the American hospital in Beirut.

The lights go down, and Nina Simone's 'Sinnerman' plays again. Noun cries out the words along with Nina Simone.

5.

The lights go up. Noun is crouching on the floor. She crawls forward and talks to the audience as if she is afraid, or trying to hide from something. She describes life in her apartment as if she were back there again.

I was living right on the demarcation line, the border that split Beirut in two. The city centre was a pile of rubble over-run by untended trees and wild dogs.

She remembers those moments, she sees the dogs, hears them howling; she relives all those moments when they were shut away in their apartment. She smiles.

We laughed a lot back then.

She bursts out laughing.

You couldn't just turn a light on when you felt like it, because there were lone snipers watching out for shadows on the walls. Once a friend of mine lit up a cigarette in the dark without thinking. She got a bullet in the bum.

She laughs.

For nothing.

She hits the floor and stands up.

Oh, war is so pointless!

She moves closer to the audience to explain what it was like. She describes her life back then.

I spent the nights in West Beirut, in Hamra, at a club called the Backstreet. There was coke everywhere, I'd dance like I'd lost my mind, people were having sex in the toilets and snorting lines straight off the bar.

She spits out these moments, just as she lived them, in all their violence and craziness.

In the car park there was a pistachio green Chevrolet. It had red leather seats, and it was for couples who didn't fancy the toilets.

She says all this matter-of-factly, neither hiding the details nor trying to offend, just telling it as it was.

The real romantics preferred the Carrara marble tombstones in the Greek Orthodox cemetery. In June 1982, the Israeli army invaded Lebanon to get rid of the PLO, the Palestine Liberation Organisation. They placed West Beirut under siege to get Yasser Arafat to surrender. Their aeroplanes dropped tracts down on us: "We have nothing against the Lebanese, our objective is to free you from the Palestinian terrorists".

She stops. In her heart, she knows that she wasn't a Palestinian terrorist even if she lived in the wrong neighbourhood. She sees before her all the bombs that were raining down around her, and she smiles.

East Beirut had been blocked off to us since the beginning of the war. We took an apartment in the West, near the stadium… the first target for the Israeli bombs. It was like an animated film. I was talking to my father…

She hears a sound…

when a vacuum bomb went off. There was a big whoosh of air, and a second later the walls and windows of the apartment were gone. We were suspended in mid-air on the ninth floor. Our house would be destroyed seven times.

She realises what she has just said. Seven times. She remembers the seven times that they had to rebuild the house. She can hardly believe it. She doesn't want to think about how sad it is, she doesn't want to remember that. She tries to move on by carrying on telling her story.

Every cloud has a silver lining: as the Israelis approached, the Syrian army retreated. They set their tanks back on the road to Damascus with everything they'd managed to steal in Beirut. The Syrian tanks passed below our apartment block.

She remembers the Syrians and their tanks; she saw them from the balcony with her father.

On top of the turrets they had piled up washing machines, TVs, crystal chandeliers, bikes, ironing boards, flower pots, hair salon blowdryers, fridges, and even bidets. My dad shouted at them from the balcony: "You shitty army of grasses and spies, bidet snatchers, toilet thieves!

She laughs. Exhausted, she sits down to explain what happened next.

During the siege of West Beirut, my sisters and I fell very ill. We had been without water, electricity and food for a month. Our parents decided to send us to the East. My father dropped us off in the night at the border checkpoint in the alley behind the museum.

She can see the street with its barbed wire, and she can see her father.

"Go on, my little angels, you'll be safe in the East".

How could he say that she'd be safe away from him? It made her very sad to say goodbye.

An uncle was waiting for us on the other side. We were stopped at an Israeli checkpoint. We were huddled up together on the back seat of the car, all three of us covered in dust from all the bombing. We were terrified.

Yes, these are the ones who had been bombing them, standing there on top of the blockade. The dust on her skin is from their bombs.

We were sure the Israelis would cut us up into a thousand tiny pieces. But no, they gave us sweets and sent us on our way...

In her head she's thinking that after all those bombs, now they're giving us sweets.

To take our mind off things, our uncle organised a party in our honour. They held the party on the terrace of the building that overlooks the bay of Beirut.

She remembers the sights and sounds of that evening. She sees that terrace and the bay of Beirut. That's where her parents were, over there across the bay.

There was music, a huge buffet, and a belly dancer. The belly dancer shimmied away. The women were dripping head to toe in Cartier jewellery. They were in ecstasy at the sight of all the bombs raining down on West Beirut.

She is overcome by the same rage that she felt when she saw how happy they were, all around her, in those moments when the bay was being bombed, and her parents were right in the middle of it.

West Beirut was in flames. In East Beirut, couples were slow-dancing to Julio Iglesias.

She sings "Je n'ai pas changé", mimicking Julio Iglesias's accent, with all the irony and all the hypocrisy that she saw in that moment.

My sisters and I took one look at each other and we made a run for it. We ran through the night towards the museum. We got past the Israeli blockades before being frisked like drug dealers by the phalangists.

She crawls forwards on her knees, and explains what happened.

We jumped over spikes and barbed wire, and finally we were back on the other side, in West Beirut.

She falls silent. She can see it all again.

In the midst of the smoking shells of buildings there wasn't a single light, not a drop of water, not a crumb of bread, but we were happy, we were home.

She can smell the streets, and the odour of gunpowder that pervaded them.

In the next 72 hours West Beirut would be bombed more than any other city had ever been bombed. The worst part of the Israeli invasion wasn't the bombs, though, or the lack of food and water. I went for two months without a shower, my skin was grey, I looked like…

She sees the grey hue of her skin

…a tyre on a Peugeot 504. One evening, my dad gave me a

watermelon. I squeezed it so I could wash myself with the juice! No, the real calamity during the war was Italy knocking out Brazil in the World Cup in Spain, by three goals to two.

She is annoyed as she remembers what happened.

Since there was no electricity, I used to steal car batteries to power a little black and white TV set. I was in the middle of a deserted street, F-16s were flying low over the apartment buildings.

She sees the F-16s.

They were dropping cluster bombs but I didn't even care. I was focussed on the game, I only had eyes for the team in the green and gold strip. One day I'll forget the bombs, but the look on the faces of Sócrates, Paulo Isidoro, Falcão and Zico, that I'll never forget.

The lights go down. Nina Simone's 'Sinnerman' starts up again, and Noun sings along.

6.

Noun is sitting in the middle of her chalk square, and lights a candle. At the same time, the lights go up. She plays with the candle, and remembers other times when she used to do the same thing.

After all those bombs, after all that madness, from the moment when the war became truly insane…

she looks at the audience…

I started to grow up.

She is overwhelmed by the fact of remembering that wartime was all she'd ever known, that she had grown up in a time of war.

I'm sure that anyone who has lived through a war dreams of nothing but the war.

She remembers the war, the dreams that wake her almost every night, even now. She remembers the lights she saw and the sounds she heard.

The sound of it, and the lights, the lights in wartime are like nothing on earth. There were dogs too, and rats.

She bursts out laughing. She can hear the scrabbling of rats.

Rats that were so big… when they scuttled by, you'd think they were horses.

Scared, she bursts out laughing.

But the dogs, that was something else.

She can see them even now, and she is still afraid.

They'd go around in packs. In every area, there was a tribe of dogs. Their job was to eat the dead. They were huge, they had a rasping bark like nothing I'd heard before. They weren't like ordinary dogs, they didn't walk the same, their eyes, their bark were strange. At the end of the war, all dogs were exterminated. They had eaten too many Lebanese people.

She bursts out laughing. She remembers the things they used to say to each other, laughing, in the midst of all that carnage.

It was such a farce, that war: Lina, my neighbour, would happily stand up to the soldiers, and carry on doing her shopping even in the middle of a bomb raid. She used to laugh when the Israeli F-16s flew overhead, but if she came home at night and found a cockroach in her apartment, she'd let out a scream that would wake up the whole neighbourhood.

She laughs.

We'd jump out of bed to go to her rescue. She ended up getting hit by a stray bomb. I went to see her in hospital a few hours before she died. She was laughing. There was only one thing on her mind.

She hears Lina's voice:

"Hey, Noun, what if there really is life after death? Who's going to get us our weed up there?"

Smiling, she can see herself back in the hospital with her friend.

I slipped a gram into her hand. She closed her eyes one last time, she died at peace.

She looks at the audience and returns to her story about the war.

I felt like a rat, or like one of the stray dogs. You should have seen how we moved about in the night, in the back alleys, in the darkness.

She sees herself going down flights of steps, creeping into streets and buildings. Even in the pitch dark they could find their way around.

In seventeen years of war, there were no streetlights in Beirut. I learnt to get around in the dark, I found myself in the strangest places. We all knew each other, but yet we didn't: we were just living the same madness. I lived on the battle line, I started hanging out with the militiamen, I'd go down to see them every night. They had fires, weapons, alcohol.

She plays with the candle flame. She sees the moments she lived through, those nights, those lights, those places, those streets, those faces, those soldiers.

There was no foreplay, no pretext, no desire, no words, it was just that, crude as it was: we'd fuck to have a fag, we'd fuck just to fuck, we'd fuck because there was a moment of calm, we'd fuck to forget about the bullets flying over our heads, we'd fuck while we were waiting for the pasta to cook.

Half sitting, she brings her face closer to the candle.

Every three months, I went off to Cyprus to see my father. We'd always meet in the same bar, and he'd sit with his head hunched over his drink.

She can see him now.

I could just see a vein in his forehead start to throb, while I threw everything at him: drugs, sex, the death I saw all around me, and he never judged. He didn't believe in guilt, and used to say that no-one should ever feel guilt for doing what they want. I wanted to see how much he could take.

She smiles. She sees herself with him.

There were times... we loved getting drunk together. We'd dance in the streets.

She sees the streets of all the cities he had lived in, when they used to walk back home together.

He'd say he was worried because sexually I was doing the same things as him. I'd tell him all about my conquests, I was fascinated by dicks. I'd seen lopsided ones, dead straight ones, puffed-up ones and trussed-up ones, bracelets, gimlets, giblets, ringlets, wolverines, jelly beans, fudge cakes without the fudge.

With every term, she sees the penis that matches the image.

Peaky ones, cheeky ones, floppy ones, stroppy ones, light sabres, tomb raiders, space invaders and caped crusaders. Hedgehogs, woodpeckers, hot dogs, double deckers, sandbaggers, jackhammers, poker faces and Amazing Graces. I didn't like uncircumcised dicks, I used to play with the foreskin, pulling it down like a catapult.

"OK Pappa, you know everything, what do you do with that

floppy bit at the end?"

He was sitting on the terrace of the Samurai lounge bar in Nicosia, he downed his glass of arak in one, and then burst out laughing.

She can hear his voice.

"Noun, you take uncircumcised dicks by their tip, and you blow as hard as you can, as if you were playing a saxophone. Tomorrow I'll sign you up to a music class."

She blows out the candle. The lights go down. Nina Simone's 'Sinnerman' plays again, Noun sings along.

7.

The lights come up. Noun is sitting down in a corner of the square.

It was like living with the contrast turned up, that was just life, no questions asked, that was the name of the game! We didn't take anything seriously, not even death. I got married for the first time on a whim, or rather on the back of a prang. It was summer in Beirut, I was driving down towards Clemenceau street, this bloke drove into the back of me. We swapped numbers. A week later, he asked me to marry him. He was a war photographer, and his name was…

She pauses, it's as if in saying his name aloud she's going to relive everything she went through with him.

…Marwan.

She sees Marwan's face as clearly as if he were there in front of her now.

Marwan would leave early in the morning to hunt down corpses, sometimes he'd even take a picture of himself with his friends after one of them had been shot. What was I thinking, living with a war photographer in the middle of a war?

She remembers how crazy it was, all those moments she lived through with him, and what she put herself through.

He threw himself into the violence of the war, he lived on the edge of the abyss and that was how he made his living. He carried the war inside him, in his body and in his soul. When he came back from a day's work he wouldn't sleep, he was incapable of getting back to any kind of normal life. He was always after another war, and if he couldn't find one he'd make one. You should have seen how excited he'd get when the shooting got closer to our building. Every time he heard a missile he had to run out onto the balcony so that he didn't miss a thing, and I'd shout out to him:

She sees herself back there, in that apartment with Marwan.

"My love, I'm not afraid of dying, but please, not like this!"

I'd become addicted to war, just like him.

This utterance drops from her lips as if it were sentencing her.

I set up a dark room in the apartment and I used to develop his photos of the dead. There was just the red light, the developing tray and the fixing tray. The photo paper that I would push down into the liquid…

Suddenly she's back in that dark room with those chemical smells.

… and the outlines of blown-up bodies that would come to the surface little by little, like magic… Marwan was violent without even realising it. He went from one mass grave to the next, from one massacre to the next, fucking anyone and anywhere. He would bring home one infection after another and my body couldn't cope any more. I shut down from him. He didn't understand, and so he'd hit me as hard as he could. To deal with all the filth that was his daily bread, he became a clean freak at home. I wasn't allowed to leave the tiniest little fingerprint on the chrome handle of the fridge, otherwise I'd get a punch in the face. His biggest obsession was how his shirts were ironed. There couldn't be a single crease visible to the naked eye, and the hangers had to be spaced at least ten centimetres apart, otherwise I'd get a good beating. The worst thing of all was the ritual of the bedsheets. He wanted them changed every day. He made me pin them to the underside of the mattress so they wouldn't get crumpled in the night.

The memory of this duty is more painful to her than all the rest.

The number of pins I stabbed into my fingers… I had permanent bruises all over my hands. One night of heavy bombing, he had taken LSD; I had just found out I was pregnant.

Obviously, it wasn't good news.

I was in the bedroom, I had pulled the bed away from the wall to change the sheets. He wanted to have sex. I said no. He went ballistic. Seeing that I was between the bed and the wall, he grabbed hold of the headboard and started smashing it into my stomach. The third time it hit me, I felt something burst, here.

She hits her stomach with her hands, as if to remind herself of what she felt at that moment.

I was trapped between the bed and the wall, naked, bleeding

life out of me, but I was happy, I wasn't thinking about anything, I just wanted to hear the last of the bomb blasts in the Beirut night. I had just turned seventeen.

It's a shock to her that she was only seventeen years old and yet she was living through all that.

It's strange, that desire for violence, as if the violence of the war wasn't enough. We were almost as criminal as the people who went around killing each other. We didn't have guns or machetes, but we were so twisted with ourselves, with each other, pushing one another to do the craziest things!

She brings herself back to the audience to carry on telling them about her life with this man, her first husband.

I was afraid of being alone, so I went out to find Marwan and bring him back home.

She is not proud of what she has just said, and she wasn't proud of it when it happened either.

My dad, who knew nothing about all this, called me from Cyprus.

She can hear her father's voice.

"If you don't leave that man, that wife-beater, I won't have anything more to do with you, you'll be dead to me".

That's it, that's what she needed, an ultimatum that made her realise what she was allowing her husband to put her through. Thank goodness her father was always there for her.

I got over Marwan, and got on with my life. I fell in love with Ramzi, a brilliant musician who lived in West Beirut. There were three of us: me, Ramzi, and Hussein. We'd smoke, drink, listen to music… We used to do free base.

The simple fact of saying the words 'free base' makes her remember the smell of that drug, the things it made her feel, things she never wants to feel again, and their consequences. She sees the room, the apartment, she sees herself with Ramzi.

One night, Hussein said he wanted to leave Lebanon. We didn't understand why someone would ever want to leave such an amazing country. We spent two full days talking. They knew I always had a gun on me. Ramzi asked for the gun. I got it out. He smiled, and said:

"Let's play Russian Roulette for the next round of hits. The loser leaves theirs for the next player."

She can hardly breathe. She sees now how crazy they were.

We must have had at least fifty grams of coke to last three nights. Hussein was freaking out, he was too far gone, we sat around the table. Ramzi went first and click, nothing.

She sees the gun, passing from one hand to another, and she hears the sound of the cylinder turning.

The next player had to turn the cylinder and then pull the trigger. Hussein had a go, then me. The bullet stayed in the cylinder. I wasn't afraid, it was exciting, I felt as if I was going to come. We took a break after every turn. When you come out of it alive, you don't talk, you just look at each other, you get up, take another hit, start talking about what you're feeling, and then you end up laughing like hyenas. It was like *The Deer Hunter*. The most intense thing about Russian Roulette is the way the others look at you, their surprise when you pull the trigger and nothing happens. It stays with you. Each time we took the gun, we had to turn the cylinder and pull the trigger. Hussein did it again. He passed me the gun. I laughed at Ramzi, sweating as if it was his turn. Hussein shouted:

"I want to leave this fucking country!"

Ramzi was preparing the next hit, to take or to lose. He tried to calm Hussein down.

"Don't say that, Lebanon is amazing".

I passed the gun to Ramzi. He forgot to spin the cylinder. He teased Hussein:

"Come on, you can't leave, Lebanon is amazi…"

And he pulled the trigger. I saw his brain burst out of his skull.

Noun falls to the floor, and caves in on herself. It's the only time she cries. The only moment when you really feel that this war has destroyed her. That they were all destroying each other. Even when death wasn't seeking them out, they went courting it. This is the moment of absolute tragedy for her. She sees Ramzi. She sees him dead. She sees his brain splattered across the room, and she sees how inhuman they had become, and how that war had turned them all into monsters. The lights go down. Nina Simone's 'Sinnerman' plays again, but this time Noun screams the words as she never has before.

8.

When the lights come back up, Noun is still singing her heart out in the middle of the chalk square. She realises that the lights have come up, and stops short. She looks at the audience, and carries on telling her story.

My father decided to leave Cyprus after nine years in exile, and come back to Beirut.

She moves towards the front of the stage.

We were happy to have him back, but he didn't feel safe. The Syrian secret service was everywhere.

She is afraid, and starts drawing back slowly.

One morning in June, he packed his briefcase meticulously, and put his gun in his pocket. He never went anywhere without it. In the street below, he felt something wasn't right. Someone greeted him before putting a silencer to his head. I heard screams outside, I ran out onto the balcony. Our neighbour shouted up to me: "They got your dad with a silencer!" I saw my dad lying on his back in a pool of blood. Everything was red, his clothes, his briefcase, the pavement. I whispered "he's dead, he's dead." The emergency services got there quickly, and he was still alive. The doctors managed to extract the bullet from his brain. Twenty days later he came out of his coma, but he could hardly see, he could hardly hear.

She comes back to the edge of the stage, towards the audience.

Years later, tired of being on the run, weakened by his ill health, he tried to get his Syrian passport back. He wasn't well and didn't think he was a threat to anyone any more.

She starts to draw back again.

I was living in Damascus, I went knocking on every door to try to get him his passport back. I brought him to Damascus, the officials there assured me that they just needed to ask him one or two questions. We ended up at the headquarters of the Secret Services. For a week they took him for interrogation every morning, let him out for an afternoon break, only to bring him back for interrogation until midnight. In the end, they decided to lock him up. They put him in a glass cell; they didn't torture him, no-one dared touch him, he was too famous.

She looks directly at the audience.

But they rigged up loudspeakers that streamed an uninterrupted soundtrack of the screams of the men they were torturing in the neighbouring cells.

The lights go down, and Nina Simone's 'Sinnerman' comes on again. Noun belts out the song.

9.

*The lights come back up. Noun is still singing her heart out alone.
She is crouching in a corner of the chalk square, covering her ears
with her hands. She calls out to her father.*

Can you hear them Pappa? They're breaking down the door.
We don't have much time left. I've told my story.

*She takes her hands away from her ears. She tries to speak in a more
normal voice. She tries to talk to him.*

I thought I'd said everything. And now what am I to do? Tell
me!

She beats the floor with her hands. She wants answers.

I thought about all those years, your dreams, your delusions,
your principles, your failures. And now I wonder if you didn't
just use me like a lab rat, if I wasn't just a test tube where you
could try out your wildest dreams.

She shouts at him, unleashing all her rage on her father.

Do you know what I think? I think you forgot I was your daughter, otherwise you'd never have done any of it!

She can hear the men beating at the door.

They're breaking the door down Pappa, what am I going to do now with your fucking freedom in this fucking country?

She shouts at him, screams at him.

You didn't give me freedom, you gave me a poisoned chalice. How could I be free all on my own surrounded by millions of lunatics? I don't know how you couldn't see that.

She remembers something.

You did, though, you did see it, on your deathbed.

She remembers her father's words.

"Noun, I think I've lost, don't stay here, get out. Go to Paris".

She hits the floor even harder than before.

It was too late, Pappa!

She shouts.

You didn't see our country was losing its freedom because you were so busy dreaming about mine. I said I'd told you everything, but there are things I hid from you.

She calms down and talks to him.

I had the right to keep some things to myself, but now you need to know.

She starts to tell her father what happened to her.

At the end of the war, I was performing Kafka at university. Men with beards came into the theatre, rolled out their rugs on the stage, and started to pray. I kicked them up the backside. They tied me to a chair and hit me a thousand and one times with a metal ruler, here, on my knees, until they were just blood and bone.

She starts to get upset and to cry, but she doesn't want to give in to tears, she's a fighter.

I went back home, I wasn't crying, I was furious. I stopped off at Mazen's chemist's. I asked for the strongest poison they had, to kill the biggest rat imaginable. They gave me a kitsch-looking Indian thing in a red, yellow and blue packet.

She can see the packet of poison, and remembers walking down the street towards home.

You were having your afternoon nap. You used to love it when I made a Turkish coffee for you when you woke up.

She can smell the aroma of the coffee.

I tipped all the poison into your coffee. You took a sip, and said it tasted strange. I told you it was fine, it was just the chlorine in the water. Since you trusted me blindly, you knocked the whole lot back in one gulp.

She realises what she has done, and she is afraid.

You put on your hat. I watched you from the balcony, saying to myself "he's going to croak, he's going to croak." But you didn't, you just carried on walking as if nothing had happened.

She is annoyed.

You came home in a good mood that evening, though you did mention a mild diarrhoea.

She is irritated.

In the night I was woken up by the pain in my knees. I hated you for it, I still wanted to kill you. I took the gun out of your briefcase. I wanted to make your murder look like a suicide, because you had so many reasons to want to kill yourself. I went and got my mother's pink rubber washing up gloves.

She can see the scene and hear the sounds.

I crept up to you silently. You were asleep in the living room. You were snoring and talking in your sleep. I pressed the gun against your forehead and, just when I was about to pull the trigger, I saw the ridiculous pink glove I was wearing and I felt like killing my mother instead, but she was out that night.

She kneels down and says threateningly to her father:

Lucky for you, Pappa!

The lights go down, and Nina Simone's 'Sinnerman' starts up again. Noun sings louder than ever.

10.

The lights come back up. Noun is singing the last words of the song, 'Sinnerman', shouting them out. She folds her arms across her chest, clasping each hand around the opposite shoulder. She speaks to her father. Everything she has said up until now has been building up to this point: to tell her father what happened to her.

My beloved Pappa, I'm writing to you in the air. I'm writing to you from a place where writing is forbidden. In this last month I've learnt to write in the air. Forgive me, I wasn't able to go to your funeral. They said that a woman can't go to a burial, because women are not worthy of death.

This makes her angry, of course.

Forgive me, I didn't manage to have you buried with your face turned towards the sky. They said that all men must be buried lying on their right hand side, with their faces turned towards Mecca.

She's beside herself thinking about what they did to him, that they buried him on his right hand side with his face turned to Mecca. She knows that it was exactly what he hadn't wanted. She knows that she owes him an apology because she didn't stop them from doing it.

Forgive me, I didn't manage to get you buried where you wanted, in Salamiyeh, where you were born.

Now she has a lump in her throat. It's true, she couldn't carry out his final wish.

The officials in Damascus said: "the body of that enemy of God will never defile Syrian soil."

She mocks the voices of the Syrian secret servicemen as she repeats their words.

The day after your funeral, I went to the Babylon bar, and I ordered a Bloody Mary without the vodka.

She can see the bar where she ordered the drink, and the people there, and the DJ.

I wanted to dance myself into oblivion, dance until I could forget myself. I nodded to the DJ, he knew me. He put on Nina Simone's 'Sinnerman'.

It's her favourite song. The song plays again from the beginning and Noun moves forward towards the front of the stage. She is speaking over the music.

It was winter in Beirut. It was raining. I used to like dancing topless. I almost lifted up my t-shirt to pull it off. I felt a hand grab hold of me by my hair. It was my brother-in-law. He pulled me around the dance floor three times, dragging me along the floor by my hair. The people there pretended they couldn't see me, they stepped over me and carried on dancing to the music of Nina Simone. Some of them even applauded.

"She thought she was such a star, it's about time a man put her back in her place".

She recounts these events simply. She describes them frankly, in all their brutality, with all the rage that is inside her.

Still dragging me by the hair, he pulled me down a stone stairwell. I felt my ribs smash against the steps. I was screaming my head off. No-one lifted a finger in that nightclub where I'd practically grown up. My sister reassured the clientele.

She imitates her sister.

"My father didn't do a very good job raising her, it's down to us now." Out in the street, her husband tried to force me into his car. I bent backwards with all my might, and kicked so hard I broke the side window. That made him lose it completely. He shoved my head into the gutter. A bouncer tried to intervene.

"What's up with you? Are you crazy, you're beating up a girl! Leave her alone.

My brother-in-law replied:

"Do you know what this bitch said?"

"No".

"She said she pissed on God".

The bouncer put me in a choke hold.

"There you go, brother, give the bitch what she deserves".

She sees herself back there, and everything those men did to her.

My brother-in-law started raining punches down on me. Then he pushed me up against a barbed wire fence. I could feel the sharp ends ripping at my back. He was hitting me over and over, as if he had lost control. I fell to the ground. Before I lost consciousness I felt him wipe his feet on my body and on my face. When I opened my eyes I was back at home, in a heap on the floor. My first thought was to run to the bathroom to see what they had done to me. I stood in front of the mirror. I lifted my head up slowly.

She lifts her head.

I looked at myself as if I was a camera, as if I was the mirror. When I saw my reflection, I screamed.

She sees herself in the mirror and she screams.

Ya ékhouètte ésharmoutta, Baba! Son of a bitch, Pappa!

The music stops. She calls out to her father with all the sorrow that she had felt when she saw herself in the mirror, when she saw her face and what they had done to her. She is stunned.

I could hardly recognise myself. My right eye was smashed in, it was dark purple and completely bloodshot. There was blood running out of my eardrum, two of my ribs were broken, there was mud all over my face, and there were gashes on my back from the barbed wire. I had his footprints on my face.

She can hardly believe what she's describing to her father, what she sees in the mirror. She refuses to believe what she sees in the mirror, it's not possible.

I was admitted to the emergency room of the Greek Orthodox hospital. I got my phone out. I wanted to wake up the whole of Beirut. Nurses arrived in the middle of the night, they snatched my phone from me and pulled the landline out of the socket. The doctor on duty smiled when I told him what had happened to me. He pressed a button. Three huge male nurses burst into the room. They pinned me to the bed and stabbed a tranquilliser needle into me. I half opened my eyes. I was in an ambulance.

She thought she was free because she was on the move.

I couldn't move, they'd put me...

Now she shouts out what they did to her.

...in a straitjacket!

She collapses in on herself, then stands up slowly, lifts her head and sees exactly what she saw at that moment.

I watched the lights of Beirut go by. Everything seemed round: the buildings, the streets, the cars. Beside me, I could hear my mother crying as if she was far away. She was praying at the same time:

"Dear Lord, please don't let my daughter become a whore, she smokes marijuana and shows her breasts in public. Dear Lord, she's mad, please heal her".

My sister was at her side.

She would never have believed it. These people were supposed to defend her and protect her. She can't believe what's happening to her.

The ambulance stopped in a park. I had just arrived at the Convent of the Holy Cross, Dayr Assalibe, the mental asylum in Jounieh. We were taken to one of the nuns, in an office with icons of the Blessed Virgin everywhere. I was still in the straitjacket. I was just coming round from the morphine. The nun brought out a piece of paper:

"Madam, I need the signatures of three relatives who will certify that your daughter is mad".

She can see her mother now.

My mother replied in a low voice:

"My daughter and I are here, and her uncle will sign too. I'm worried for my son-in-law".

Noun cannot believe what she is hearing.

The nun reassured her.

"Don't worry about the complaint she filed against her brother-in-law. Lebanese law states that in the absence of the father, every man in the family is responsible for correcting the behaviour of a deviant woman. He was only doing his duty".

Noun takes all this in.

"May God put her back on the right path" said my mother, my sister and my uncle before they scarpered.

She addresses her father, her arms still wrapped across her chest.

I was left alone, in the middle of the park, in my straitjacket.

Her arms have become the straitjacket. She tries to make light of the situation, so as not to make her father too upset by what she has just said.

This you didn't see…

This you didn't know…

Maybe it's better that way…

On the outside

They had all decided

I was a public menace…

A danger to society…

Me!!

She smiles.

And the rest of them?!!!

The killers

The snipers

The thieves

The rapists

The soldiers

The fundamentalists

All of them are of sound mind

And on the loose out there!

And I'm shut up in here

And mad…

She whispers.

That's what they did to me.

That was the price.

In the lunatic asylum, in the women's ward, writing was forbidden. And so I learnt to write in the air, Pappa. All day long, I would write: "Lebanon is sovereign, democratic, and free." I'm writing in the air now, Pappa, all these words are just air, Pappa, our war was nothing but air, all our love stories… only air. Our freedom was just air too, Pappa, and above all your dreams… they were nothing but air. Pappa, I love you.

She recites her father's favourite poem and sees him there before her. She opens up her arms, freeing herself from her straitjacket, and goes towards her father repeating the poem again. The lights start to fade.

"Your heart wanders from one love to the next
But you'll never forget your first love.
You'll make many homes for yourself on this earth
But you'll never forget your first home."

The lights fade out as she continues walking to the edge of her square. She finishes the poem, reciting the final lines in the darkness.

Naked Eye Publishing

A fresh approach

Naked Eye Publishing is an independent not-for-profit micro-press intent on publishing quality poetry and literature, including in translation.

A particular focus is translation. We aim to take a midwife role in facilitating the translation of works that have until now been disregarded by English-language publishing. We will be happy if we function purely as an initial stepping-stone both for overlooked writers and first-time literary translators.

Each of us at Naked Eye is a volunteer, competent and professional in our work practice, and not intending to make a profit for the press. We see ourselves as part of the revolution in book publishing, embodying the newly levelled playing field, sidestepping the publishing establishment to produce beautiful books at an affordable price with writers gaining maximum benefit from sales.

nakedeyepublishing.co.uk